MaMMals

Please visit our web site at: **www.garethstevens.com**
For a free color catalog describing Gareth Stevens Publishing's list of high-quality books and multimedia programs, call 1-800-542-2595 (USA) or 1-800-387-3178 (Canada). Gareth Stevens Publishing's fax: (414) 332-3567.

Library of Congress Cataloging-in-Publication Data

Hair-raising, the mammal files.
    Mammals.
        p. cm. — (Discovery Channel school science: the plant and animal kingdoms)
    Contents: Mammals—Ch-ch-ch-ch-changes—Growing up mammal—Order, please—The Mammal Hall of Fame—SPOTlight on a predator—Never cry wolf, by Farley Mowat—Life among the chimps, by Jane Goodall—Magnificent marsupials and marvelous monotremes—(Not) alone in the dark—Mammal or not?—No offense, but you really smell—Saving the Florida panther—Call of the wild—Mammal mania—The last living mammal.
    ISBN 0-8368-3217-5 (lib. bdg.)
    1. Mammals—Juvenile literature. [1. Mammals.] I. Title. II. Series.
QL706.2.H35   2002
599—dc21   2002021194

This edition first published in 2002 by
Gareth Stevens Publishing
A World Almanac Education Group Company
330 West Olive Street, Suite 100
Milwaukee, WI 53212 USA

Writers: Steven Otfinoski, Lynn Brunelle

Editors: Jackie Ball, Marc Gave

Photographs: Cover, © Corel; pp. 2-3 © Corel; p. 6, © Corel; p. 7, polar bear, dolphins, and whale © Corel; p. 7, arctic fox, © Norbert Rosing/Animals Animals; p. 7, bat-eared foxes, © Terry G. Murphy/Animals Animals; p. 9 (both), © Corel; p. 12, tiger, © Corel; p. 12, three-toed sloth, © Michael Fogden/Animals Animals; p. 13, woman with long hair, © Bettmann/CORBIS; p. 13, dolphin and giraffe © Corel; pp. 14-15, leopard, © Corel; pp. 16-17, © Corel; p. 18, Jane Goodall, Michael Nichols/NSG Image Collection; p. 19, chimpanzee, © A. & M. Shah/Animals Animals; pp. 20-21, echidna and platypus, © Fritz Prenzel/Animals Animals; pp. 20-21, numbat, © Goodale, R.J.B. OSF/Animals Animals; pp. 20-21, quokka © Nielson, L. OSF/Animals Animals; pp. 20-21, tasmanian devil, © Hans & Judy

This U.S. edition © 2002 by Gareth Stevens, Inc. First published in 1999 as *Hair-raising: The Mammal Files* by Discovery Enterprises, LLC, Bethesda, Maryland. © 1999 by Discovery Communications, Inc.

Further resources for students and educators available at www.discoveryschool.com

Designed by Bill SMITH STUDIO
Designers: Eric Hoffsten, Jay Jaffe, Brian Kobberger, Nick Stone, Sonia Gauba
Photo Editor: Justine Price
Art Buyer: Lillie Caporlingua
Gareth Stevens Editor: Alan Wachtel
Gareth Stevens Art Director: Tammy Gruenewald

Beste/Animals Animals; pp. 24-25 (both), © Raymond A. Mendez/Animals Animals; p. 26, bloodhound, © Corel; p. 27, bloodhound sniffing, © Kent & Donna Dannen; pp. 28-29 (both), © Corel; p. 30, star-nosed mole, © Michael Habicht/Animals Animals; p. 30, elephant, © Corel.

Illustrations: pp. 4-5, 22-23, Dianne Gaspas and Patricia J. Wynne.

Acknowledgements: Excerpts from NEVER CRY WOLF by Farley Mowat. Copyright © 1963 by Farley Mowat Limited; copyright © renewed 1991 by Farley Mowat Limited. By permission of Little Brown and Co. Inc. Excerpts from THROUGH A WINDOW by Jane Goodall. Copyright © 1990 by Soko Publications Ltd. Reprinted by permission of Houghton Mifflin Co. All rights reserved. Interview with David and Hilda Onderdonk from EVERY CREEPING THING by Richard Conniff. Copyright © 1998 by Henry Holt and Company Inc. Excerpts reprinted by permission.

CONTENTS

You Animal

There was a day, not too long ago in geological terms, when the only mammals were tiny shrewlike animals cowering beneath the grass as the thundering footsteps of dinosaurs rocked their world.

Now look! Mammals are everywhere, and they come in a fabulous array of shapes and sizes, habits and means of locomotion.

In MAMMALS, Discovery Channel explores the world of mammals and humans' special connection with our animal "classmates." The more we know about mammals, the more we know about ourselves and our world.

MAMMALS

Mammals . . . 4
At-a-Glance
Everything you need to know about being a mammal. You are one, after all. Refer back to this page again and again.

These mammals live in the ocean.
See page 7

Final Project

Mammals

Mammals. You know them, you love them, and you're one of them. Humans share the planet with about 4,000 other species of mammals, from the thumb-sized pygmy shrew to the three-times-as-long-as-a-city-bus blue whale.

Not every creature, of course, is a mammal. There are only two requirements: hair and milk from mammary glands. But most mammals have other features in common, too.

**FEATURE:
DIFFERENTIATED TEETH**
Many mammals have different kinds of teeth for different tasks.

FEATURE: BLUBBER
An adaptation unique to polar bears, whales, and some other mammals, blubber is a layer of insulating fat beneath the skin.

There are three different kinds of mammals:

PLACENTAL—Those nourished inside their mother's uterus through a placenta

MARSUPIAL—Those developed in a uterus but sheltered and fed in their mother's pouch

MONOTREMES—Those developed in eggs

FEATURE: A BACKBONE
You have to have a backbone to be a mammal, but just because you have one doesn't automatically make you a mammal. Fish and frogs have them, too.

FEATURE: FOUR LIMBS
Mammals can have two legs and two arms, four legs, or a pair each of flippers and fins.

REQUIREMENT: HAIR
Some have more than others, but all mammals have some hair. Cats, dogs, horses, bears, and weasels generally have more hair on their bodies than people have (well, most people) and more than dolphins and whales. But every mammal has some hair, in some form or another, at some time of its life. Mammals that live in cold climates, such as polar bears, have long hollow hairs for insulation.

REQUIREMENT: NURSING BABIES WITH MILK FROM MAMMARY GLANDS
The words mammal and mammary sound alike because they're related. This characteristic is strictly a mammal thing.

FEATURE: WARM BLOOD
If you're a mammal, you're endothermic, or warm-blooded. This means that your body temperature stays pretty much the same no matter whether you find yourself in the snow or in the sun. Being endothermic rules out amphibians, fish, and modern reptiles, whose body temperatures are regulated by their environments. They're exothermic, or cold-blooded.

FEATURE: GIVING BIRTH TO LIVE YOUNG
The great majority of mammals don't lay eggs. Mammal babies develop inside the mother and then are born. There are a few exceptions; the duck-billed platypus and the echidna are two mammals that lay eggs, and there are a few kinds of snakes that give birth to live young. But generally, if your baby doesn't hatch out of an egg outside its mother's body, you probably are a mammal.

5

Ch-ch-ch-ch-changes

Over billions of years, our planet has undergone quite a few changes. Environments have cooled down, heated up, gotten wetter, and gotten drier. Oceans, deserts, forests, grasslands, tundra, mountains, and beaches have come and gone. And with these changes have come new species of animals and plants that have changed, or adapted, to live in these conditions and ecosystems. Mammals have undergone a staggering variety of changes since they first appeared on Earth. How have these changes come about? In the 1800s, there was a great debate about this question.

Paris, France, 1809

French scientist Jean-Baptiste Lamarck thought animals adapted by using body parts to fit into the conditions around them:

It is interesting to observe the result of habit in the peculiar shape and size of the giraffe (Camelo-Pardalis): this animal, the largest of the mammals, is known to live in the interior of Africa in places where the soil is nearly always arid and barren, so that it is obliged to browse on the leaves of trees and to make constant efforts to reach them. From this habit long maintained in all its race, it has resulted that the animal's fore-legs have become longer than its hind legs, and that its neck is lengthened to such a degree that the giraffe, without standing up on its hind legs, attains a height of six metres (nearly 20 feet).

Cambridge, England, 1859

Half a century later, Charles Darwin had a different idea. Darwin argued that animals changed because the environment selected the most successful traits. In other words, giraffes have long necks because those animals with long necks were the ones that survived to reproduce and pass along their long-necked genes:

It may be said that natural selection is daily and hourly scrutinizing, throughout the world, every variation, even the slightest; rejecting that which is bad, preserving and adding up all that is good; silently and insensibly working, whenever and wherever opportunity offers, at the improvement of each organic being in relation to its organic and inorganic conditions of life. We see nothing of these slow changes in progress, until the hand of time has marked the long lapses of ages, and then so imperfect is our view into long past geological ages, that we only see that the forms of life are now different from what they formerly were.

Science confirms that Darwin was right. There are variations within a population, and some of these variations might help an animal survive better and pass along the genes for that particular characteristic. The process is called *natural selection*. It's what drives the gradual changes of evolution, the development over time of all living species. The examples on the next page show how certain animals have adapted.

Take a look at these two foxes, noting their differences. Why is the one on the left suited to the desert and the one on the right to the northern polar regions?

Think this bear is white? Think again. Underneath its fur, the polar bear is black. Black skin soaks up heat from the sun and helps keep the animal warm. The bear appears white because it is covered with hollow, white fur. Its hollow fur helps the polar bear float in water. In what other ways do you think this bear is adapted to its environment?

HIGH FLIERS

Bats are the only mammals that fly. How did these animals get their wings? Bat ancestors lived in trees and ate insects and fruit. Somewhere along the line, a bat was born with a flap of skin that stretched across the finger bones. Perhaps this extra skin webbing gave that bat ancestor some sort of advantage, and it reproduced and passed the characteristic on to its offspring. After generations and generations of bats, the fingers became very long and a thin membrane joined the fingers together to become wings.

UNDERWATER MAMMALS

Whales, a group that includes dolphins, are mammals that spend their lives in water. Their bodies have adapted to underwater life in a number of ways:

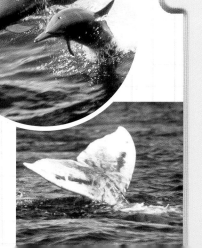

- **Bodies** are smooth and streamlined with little hair and no external ears.
- **Limbs** are strong, rigid fins and flukes that help them swim.
- **A layer of blubber beneath the skin** insulates them like a wet suit from the cold waters they live in.

Activity

START YOUR OWN SCRAPBOOK How have other mammals adapted for life today? Make an adaptation scrapbook. Cut out pictures of mammals and the environments in which they live. Make notes about why these animals look the way they do. Do their looks have anything to do with how they related to their environments? Fill your scrapbook with pictures, articles, notes, and drawings.

GROWING UP

Did you know you're related to a lizard? No, not your cousin Harold. Scientists believe mammals evolved from a group of reptilelike animals called synapsids, which lived 320 to 275 million years ago. Mammals developed from scaly creeping things to the furry creatures of all sorts we know today by adapting to a changing environment over millions and millions of years.

The development of mammals took more than just time: it took a lucky break. When this planet was ruled by enormous dinosaurs, there wasn't a lot of room for a little mammal to survive and be happy. The mammals that did exist were tiny and shy.

But then something drastic occurred to kill the dinosaurs. Many scientists believe that a huge asteroid struck the earth, sending up clouds of dust into the air. The dust clouds killed the plants that were the plant-eating dinosaurs' food source. The meat-eating dinosaurs whose main meals were the plant-eaters couldn't survive, either. But the little mammals that fed on meat had all the dinosaurs to eat. They found a way to survive and reproduce. NOW, look. Mammals are everywhere.

3,500 MILLION YEARS AGO	**500 MILLION YEARS AGO**	**360 MILLION YEARS AGO**	**AROUND 320 MILLION YEARS AGO**	**AROUND 286 MILLION YEARS AGO**	**AROUND 213 MILLION YEARS AGO**
Life is just beginning to form in the seas.	Snails and other simple animals, such as sponges and sea jellies, show up.	The first amphibians appear.	Synapsids, with jaws and teeth, appear. These animals will give rise to mammals.	The first reptiles appear.	The first dinosaurs begin to roam the earth. They will rule for over 125 million years.

MAMMAL

AROUND 160 MILLION YEARS AGO	AROUND 130 MILLION YEARS AGO	AROUND 65 MILLION YEARS AGO	AROUND 14 MILLION YEARS AGO	AROUND 4 MILLION YEARS AGO	TODAY
The first furry animals with sharp teeth and four legs appear. These are the first mammals. They're tiny and look like tree shrews.	The dinosaurs rule Earth. Mammals, such as the insect-eating *Morgan-ucodons*, thrive in the underbrush.	The dinosaurs mysteriously die out, leaving room for the mammals to take over.	Some mammals are huge! Giant creatures such as *Indricotherium*, a hornless rhinoceros that is the largest land mammal ever, wander the earth.	Hominids, the ancestors of modern humans, appear on the scene.	Mammals of many shapes and sizes walk, swim, or fly around Earth.

Activity

MAMMAL MILLENNIA Pick a mammal, any mammal, and be a time detective. Do a little digging and find out how that mammal evolved. Pick five stages of its evolutionary development and make a drawing of each stage. Under each picture write when and where the mammal lives and how it changed. End with how the mammal looks today and how it has evolved to fit the environment in which it is found.

ORDER,

All mammals have hair and nurse their young with milk. But these two traits hardly describe the great diversity between a tree shrew, an elephant, a spiny anteater, and a rhinoceros. Since their first appearance in the Triassic Period, mammals have evolved into a wide range of spectacular and not-so-spectacular animals.

The simplest way to think about the classification of mammals is to divide them into monotremes, such as the duck-billed platypus; marsupials, or pouched animals; and placental animals, which include all other living mammals. Since mammalogists find this system a bit inaccurate, it might be more precise to think of all living mammals as belonging to 20 orders. These orders are shown on the right.

This classification is not a foolproof system, though, and is always subject to change. New knowledge, or reinterpretation of old data, may further refine this system of classification. But whatever names scientists assign to them, mammals are an amazing assortment of animals.

Classification Chart

Order	Common Name
Monotremata	One hole
Marsupialia	**With a pouch**
Artiodactyla	Even-toed
Carnivora	**Flesh-eating**
Cetacea	Like whales
Chiroptera	**Hand wing**
Dermoptera	Skin wing
Hyracordea	**Like hyraxes**
Insectivora	Insect-eating
Lagomorpha	**Rabbit-shaped**
Macroscelia	Large legs
Perissodactyla	**Odd-toed**
Pholidata	Scaly ones
Pinnipedia	**Fin feet**
Primates	First
Proboscidea	**Trunk-nosed**
Rodentia	Like rodents
Sirenia	**Like sirens**
Tubulidentata	Tubular teeth
Xenarthra	**Unusual joints**

PLEASE

The Orders of Mammals

Examples	Characteristics
Platypus, spiny anteater	Lay eggs instead of giving birth to live young
Kangaroo, koala, opossum	**Rear immature offspring in abdominal pouch**
Sheep, pig, giraffe, deer, cattle, camel	Herbivorous; hooves with two or four toes
Cat, wolf, otter, weasel, bear	**Large canine teeth, clawed feet; many hunt and kill**
Whale, dolphin, porpoise	Aquatic; blowholes on top of head, front flippers
Bat	**Only flying mammals; navigate by echolocation**
Flying lemur	Fangs and wide incisors; glide from tree to tree
Hyrax	**Herbivorous; hooves and teeth like rhinoceroses**
Mole, shrew, hedgehog	Small with long snout, sharp cusped teeth
Rabbit, hare, pika	**Four upper incisors; hind legs adapted for jumping**
Elephant shrew	Shrewlike appearance with elongated nose and large back legs
Horse, zebra, tapir, rhinoceros	**Herbivorous; hooves with one or three toes**
Pangolin	Covered with horny scales; eat ants and termites
Seal, sea lion, walrus	**Marine; carnivorous; modified limbs for swimming**
Human, monkey, ape	Large brains; opposable thumbs; binocular vision
African and Asian elephants	**Large; herbivorous with trunks or elongated trunks**
Mouse, rat, beaver, squirrel	Small; herbivorous with chisel-like incisors
Dugong, manatee	**No back legs; front flippers; eat water plants in estuaries**
Aardvark	Dig up termites for food; have only four or five peglike teeth
Sloth, armadillo, anteater	**Sloths are arboreal; armadillos have scale-like covering**

Activity

CLASSIFY IT Most of us can report on the biology of cats or dogs, mammals we are familiar with. But what do you know of the dugong, the elephant shrew, the pangolin, or the tapir? Scan the examples column above and pick one animal that you know little or nothing about. Prepare a report on the biology, distribution, habits, ecology, and all other aspects of the life of this mammal. Share your information with the class.

The MAMMAL HALL of FAME

Compare a walrus to a weasel. What about a leopard to a llama? How about a person to a pig? What's the unavoidable conclusion? Mammals are full of diversity. Here are some record-setters.

LONGEST JUMPER

Kangaroos can leap up to 30 feet (9 m) in one bound.

BIGGEST MAMMAL

The blue whale, which can grow up to 100 feet (30 m) long and weigh up to 100 tons—a ton a foot! It's not only the biggest mammal, it's the biggest creature that ever lived. Even the biggest dinosaur, Brachiosaurus, was only 74 feet (23 m) long. This mighty mammal of the deep eats tiny shrimplike animals called krill—a LOT of them.

Smallest Mammal

The smallest mammal is the pygmy shrew, which measures less than two inches (5 cm) long, minus its tail. This tiny shrew is an eating machine. It burns up food so fast that if it stopped eating for half a day it would die of starvation.

NEXT 20 km

SLOWEST-MOVING MAMMAL

The sloth from South America. It moves about half a mile (.8 km) a day. Spending its entire life in the trees, the sloth hangs upside down by its hook-shaped claws, grazing on leaves. Some sloths appear green because their hair is the perfect mobile home for algae.

FLYING MAMMALS

Bats are the only mammals that can actually fly from place to place. Flying squirrels glide with the help of loose skin flaps along the sides of their bodies.

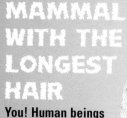

MAMMAL WITH THE LONGEST HAIR

You! Human beings win this category. If you didn't cut your hair, it would reach the floor. This goes for beards and mustaches, too. After hairy humans, musk oxen run a close second.

SWIMMING MAMMALS

Marine mammals are mammals that live in the ocean. Whales, including dolphins and porpoises, and seals are all mammals. They breathe air, but they live their lives in the water.

HIGHEST JUMPER

The puma can leap 20 feet (6 m) straight up from a standing position.

TALLEST MAMMAL

The giraffe. An adult male giraffe can reach 18 feet (5.5 m), or about three times the height of a tall human male. Amazingly, the giraffe's neck has the same number of neck bones as your neck—seven. Each one is just a lot longer. Its neck allows it to reach the tender leaves of the tallest trees, which are beyond the reach of any other herbivores.

BIGGEST LAND MAMMAL

African elephant, which can grow up to 11 feet (3.4 m) high and weigh 17,000 pounds (7,711 kg).

Activity

CLAIM TO FAME Like humans, every animal is special in its own way. Every mammal has something interesting and unique about it. To prove it, pick a letter of the alphabet at random. Then go to an encyclopedia or another source and find a mammal whose name begins with that letter. Do some research and then explain why it should belong in the Mammal Hall of Fame. Perhaps your mammal is the best smeller, has the biggest ears, can hold its breath the longest, or has the most teeth. What makes it unique? Combine some library research with firsthand observations and add this information to your scrapbook.

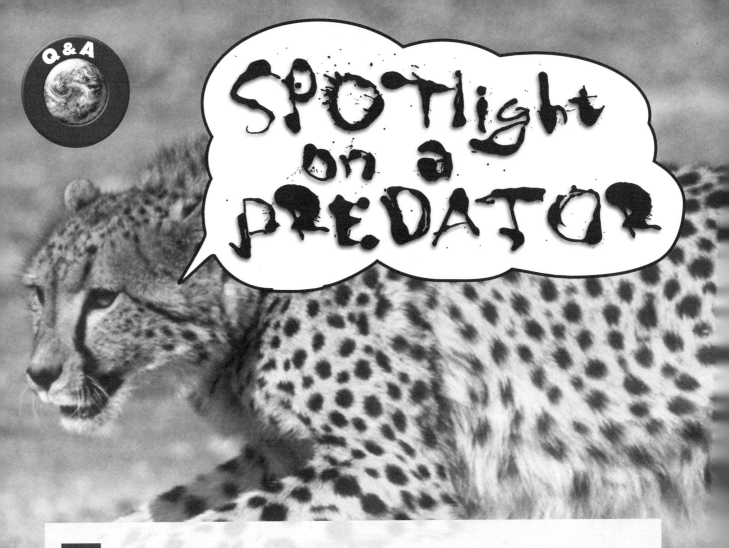

SPOTlight on a PREDATOR

The human body is designed to get energy from meat and plant food sources. We can choose to be vegetarians, but we don't have to be. Nature is more limiting for other mammals. Some mammals eat insects. Some eat plants. And others . . . well, you know what's left.

Q: You're a cheetah. Love your spots.

A: Thanks. I use 'em every day. They're more than just beauty marks, you know. They help me earn a living.

Q: What do you mean?

A: They let me blend, and blending's a beautiful thing. See, I have to sneak up on prey if I want to eat—and I DO want to eat. When I move through tall grass and brush, my spots look just like shadows in the sunlight. You can't see me coming. I can get up close and ... gotcha!

Q: I see. Very impressive. What else do you have to say about yourself?

A: Well, there are my teeth. Come over here and take a look. Come closer.

Q: Uh, well, OK. Sure. Hmm ... pretty sharp-looking!

A: Yep, and they work as well as they look. Sharp, pointy teeth are great for biting and ripping into flesh. You won't see choppers like these on some old plant-eater. Herbivores have flat teeth to chomp on grasses and grind up leaves. Works for them, but I'm a carnivore. I need meat. It's the only thing my body can use for the kind of energy I need.

Q: Any other special features I should be noticing, as long as I'm still up close? At least, for another minute?

A: My eyes. See how they face forward?

Q: How can I help it? But what does that have to do with anything?

A: Tut, tut. Everything is good for something in nature. My eyes face forward so I can scope out my territory and focus on my prey.

Q: That is interesting. Anything else?

A: Sure. I've been saving the best for last. You've probably heard about how fast I am. In fact, if I were running on most highways, I could get a ticket for speeding. I've been clocked at up to 70 miles per hour—that's almost 113 kilometers per hour. I'm built for speed, and I've got the strong, long legs to prove it. Gotta be fast to catch one of those tasty gazelles. They don't exactly dawdle, you know. Can't catch them every time, though. They're tricky. They weave back and forth trying to get away.

Q: Well, can you blame them?

A: Course not. They have their job, and I have mine. Predators try to catch prey, and prey try to get away. It's all part of the game. Plants make the energy they need from the sun. Herbivores get energy for their bodies from plants. Carnivores get energy from the flesh of these herbivores. They eat grass, we eat them—simple as that. It's the food chain, and it works for me. Of course, I'm close to the top.

Q: Is there an easy way to "spot" a prey animal?

A: The eyes can be a dead, so to speak, giveaway. Rabbits, deer, gazelles, zebras and other prey have eyes on the sides of their heads. That gives them an advantage in "spotting" danger, wherever it's coming from.

Q: What other predators are out there?

A: You've got the big cats—lions, leopards, cheetahs, bobcats, mountain lions. And then there's the canine crowd—the dogs, including wolves, wild dogs, dingoes, foxes, coyotes, and jackals. There are also hyenas, weasels, orcas, bears, and seals.

Q: What about us? Human beings?

A: Well, look at your own eyes. Not on the sides of your heads, now, are they? What do you think that means? And how about those sharp pointy teeth in the fronts of your mouths? What do you think they're for, decoration?

Q: Never thought of it that way.

A: Well, I can't blame you. You guys' hunting days are over. You just go to the supermarket, and all the meat there is already dead. But it's no disgrace to be a predator. Actually, we perform a service.

Q: How so?

A: We usually end up catching the weak, old, sick, or hurt animals. That way we weed out the weak ones and leave the strong ones to continue and reproduce. So we keep our prey strong, fast, and healthy. And the same is true for us. If we're not up to snuff in the running, hunting, and catching departments, dinner is NOT served. We don't eat, and we don't survive. Other predators get our food. So predators and prey depend on each other. We all keep each other going. You can't just remove an animal because you don't like the idea of predators. Speaking of that, I gotta run. I'm starving! See ya!

Activity

PREY TELL The cheetah has its spots for camouflage as it stalks its prey. Pick a habitat such as the East African plain and research some other features of different predators. Write about why they are effective.

NEVER CRY WOLF

Predators and prey are, over time, in a sort of ecological balance. But sometimes the balance can get tipped—or, at least, seem to. In 1963, as part of a government wildlife mission, scientist and writer Farley Mowat came to northern Canada to observe Arctic wolves. These predators were supposedly slaughtering an alarmingly high number of caribou. Ranchers feared for the safety of their cattle and sheep.

Mowat moved into a cabin in the wilderness and proceeded to get to know the wolves whose den was nearby. What he found was not what he expected, as this account of his third meeting with them shows.

The den was ... so well concealed that I was on the point of walking past without seeing it, when a series of small squeaks attracted my attention. I stopped and turned to look, and there, not fifteen feet below me, were four small, gray beasties engaged in a free-for-all wrestling match.

At first I did not recognize them for what they were. The fat, fox faces with pinprick ears; the butterball bodies, as round as pumpkins; the short, bowed legs and the tiny upthrust sprigs of tails were so far from my conception of a wolf that my brain refused to make the logical connection.

Suddenly one of the pups caught my scent. He stopped in the midst of attempting to bite off a brother's tail and turned smoky blue eyes up toward me. What he saw evidently intrigued him. Lurching free of the scrimmage, he padded toward me with a rolling, wobbly gait; but a flea bit him unexpectedly before he had gone far, and he had to sit down to scratch it.

At this instant an adult wolf let loose a full-throated howl vibrant with alarm and warning, not more than fifty yards from me.

The pups became gray streaks which vanished into the gaping darkness of the den mouth. I spun around to face the adult wolf, lost my footing, and started to skid down the loose slope toward the den.... I shot past the den mouth, over the lip of the main ridge and down the full length of the esker slope....

When I got myself straightened out and glanced back up at the esker, it was to see three adult wolves ranged side by side, all peering down at me with expressions of incredulous delight....

On three separate occasions in less than a week I had been completely at the mercy of these "savage killers" but far from attempting to tear me limb from limb, they had displayed a restraint verging on contempt, even when I invaded their home and appeared to be posing a direct threat to the young pups.

Activities

BIG BAD WOLF? Wolves have often been the subject of controversy and debate, and there is more wolf controversy now than ever. Naturalists want to reintroduce wolves to the wild in places like Montana because of deer overpopulation. But ranchers are afraid the wolves will slaughter their cattle or sheep. Do research to examine both sides of this issue and have a class debate. Use the Internet and the library for your research.

MIND OVER MYTH Farley Mowat approached the wolves with an open mind to form his own opinions. How have myths about animals contributed to what we think about them? Pick a kind of animal and, based on just your own memories and associations, make a list of words that describe what you think they're like. Then do some research about the animal's habits. Make another list and compare the two. Are the myths correct? Start with these:
- Pigs are dirty.
- Lions are noble.

LIFE AMONG

For 40 years, British zoologist Jane Goodall has been living with and studying chimpanzees in Gombe, on the shores of Lake Tanganyika in Africa. Chimpanzees are perhaps our nearest relatives in the mammal class, and Goodall has discovered, through observing their communal life, that they are more like humans than anyone thought before. In the following excerpts from her book *Through a Window*, she writes about the behavior of chimpanzees in the Kasakela community—animals to whom Goodall has given names.

Chimpanzees and humans are among the few animals that use logical thinking to solve problems. Here Goodall observes Gigi, a female chimp, as she solves the problem of how to feast on some delicious army ants without getting bitten by them.

Upon arrival at the site she [Gigi] broke a long straight branch from a nearby bush, removed the side branches, then carefully stripped the bark until she had made a smooth tool, about three feet long. She reached her hand a short way into the opening of the nest and, for a few seconds, dug frantically until the ants began to swarm out. Quickly she plunged her tool into the nest, waited for a moment, then withdrew it covered by a seething mass of ants. With rapid movements she swept the stick through her free hand, pushed the ant-mass into her mouth, and crunched vigorously. As the ants poured out of the nest in ever greater numbers, agitated by the intrusion, Gigi climbed a sapling nearby and, reaching down with her stick, continued her meal.

Like humans, chimpanzees form strong bonds of love and affection. Mothers and children are extremely close, and so are brothers and sisters, as Goodall observes in the relationship between Wolfi and his elder sister Wunda, after the death of their mother.

Wunda had carried him [Wolfi] frequently when the family travelled, not only because, like all elder sisters, she was fascinated with her small brother, but also because, from the time he was able to totter, Wolfi had wanted to follow her wherever she went. Again and again Wunda had set off about her own concerns, only to return when she heard the sad cries of her small brother as he tried, most desperately, to keep up. Then she would gather him up, and off they would go, together.

THE CHIMPS

But if chimpanzees exhibit the better traits of human beings, they also demonstrate the darker ones. In 1974, the group of chimpanzees split, for no apparent reason, into two sub-groups—the Kasakela and the Kahama. Patrols of Kasakela adults travelled along the boundaries of their territory and brutally attacked any Kahama chimpanzees they encountered. In this excerpt, six adult Kasakela males come upon a young Kahama male named Godi feeding in a tree.

Humphrey was the first to grab Godi, seizing one of his legs and throwing him to the ground. Figen, Jomeo, Sherry, and Evered pounded and stamped on their victim, while Humphrey pinned him to the ground, sitting on his head and holding his legs with both hands. Godi had no chance to escape, no chance to defend himself. Rodolf, the oldest of the Kasakela males, hit and bit at the hapless victim whenever he saw an opening …. After ten minutes Humphrey let go of Godi. The others stopped their attack and left in a noisy, boisterous group. Godi … was badly wounded, with great gashes on his face, one leg and the right side of his chest, and must have been badly bruised by the tremendous pummelling to which he had been subjected. Undoubtedly he died of his injuries, for he was never seen again by the field staff and students working in the Kahama community range.

Activity

JUST WATCH ME Keep a journal of a mammal, either a pet or another animal. Observe it closely in as many situations as possible. Write about what you see. Try to write something every day. What conclusions can you make about your mammal and the way it relates to other animals like itself, animals unlike itself, and humans?

Magnificent Marsupials and Marvelous Monotremes

There are three basic kinds of mammals. Most are placental, meaning unborn babies are nourished inside the mother's body through a membrane called the placenta. The placenta absorbs oxygen and nutrients from the mother's blood and passes them along to the embryo through the umbilical cord. This is how it happened with you; check your belly button for evidence—it's where the umbilical cord was attached to you as a fetus.

But other mammals do the baby thing a little differently. Some lay eggs. They're called monotremes, and there are only a couple of them— the duckbilled platypus and the spiny anteater, or echidna. Once the female lays her eggs, she puts them in a skin flap, or pouch, on her belly until they hatch. After they hatch, the babies stay in the pouch and nurse on her milk until they are ready to come out.

Marsupials are the third kind of mammals. They also have a pouch, but they don't lay eggs. Instead, they give birth to tiny, embryonic babies about the size of a jellybean. These jellybean babies have to make their way out of the mother's body and into the pouch on her belly, where they attach themselves to a nipple. The babies stay there for weeks or months, nursing on milk and growing. When they develop, they are ready to leave the pouch.

Only one kind of marsupial lives in America—the opossum. All the other 259 species of marsupials live in Australia and on the nearby islands of Tasmania and New Guinea.

The echidna, or spiny anteater, is about 15 inches (38 cm) long and covered with spines. The female lays one egg at a time. She deposits it into her skin flap, where it hatches and nurses until it has hair. At that point, it ventures forth out of the flap.

Duckbilled platypuses have rubbery bills and webbed feet. They also lay eggs. Kind of sounds like a bird, you say? It does. Those are birdlike qualities. But what makes this odd creature a mammal is the fact that it has fur, not feathers, and it nurses its young with milk. Only mammals nurse their young with milk.

Numbats are cat-sized marsupials that eat termites. They are covered with both spots and stripes.

Quokkas are small wallabies.

Tasmanian devils are loud, cranky little meat eaters. They are about the size of a small dog, with strong jaws and a powerful bite that they use to protect their territories from other animals.

Koalas are covered in soft, gray fur and spend their time in eucalyptus trees. They have a rounded shape, which is no accident. They're round because they have very large intestines, which they need to digest the eucalyptus leaves they eat. Koalas have pouches with the opening toward the back.

WHAT'S IN A NAME?

Check out these other wildly named marsupials:

Wombat	Chuditch
Wallaby	Wopilkara
Bandicoot	Djoongary
Cus-cus	Dibbler

(NOT) ALONE IN THE DARK

The sun has just gone down. You are wearing special glasses to help you see at night. You're cramped in this small, dark cave, but you're not alone.

There are bats everywhere—flying in and out of the entrance, hanging upside down from the cave ceiling, crouching on the cave floor. But the funny thing is that they don't seem to be making any noise. Except for the rustle of their wings flying past your ear, you can't hear anything.

The other odd thing is that even though it's dark and there are hundreds of bats flying around the cave, none of them has an accident. Watch out! A bat is heading right for you! But at the last second it steers clear.

You wouldn't know it, but the bats are making noises constantly. They make a high-pitched squeak—too high for people to hear—that allows them to "see" in the dark. This sqeaking helps them fly at night and catch insects to eat. Called echolocation, this ability works a lot like radar.

Like all sounds, the bat's squeaks have echoes. A sound goes out and then bounces off something, such as, for example, an insect. An echo is a signal to a bat, telling it exactly where an insect is. Good-bye, insect! Do you notice how few insects, blackflies, and midges there are in this cave? That's because the bats have eaten so many of them.

Bats have to catch and kill roughly half their own body weight in bugs to have enough to eat. They catch the insects as they fly and then flip the bugs into their tail membranes to eat later. Don't step on those other live insects you see at your feet—those are for dinner.

Watch your head. There's a mother nursing her baby. She's got a heavy load; at birth, the baby is already a quarter of her own weight. Luckily, her milk is extra rich, which helps the baby grow quickly. The one you're holding in your hand isn't full grown, but it's ready to fly.

DO NOT DISTURB

If it were winter, you'd see thousands of bats hanging upside down on the ceiling, sound asleep. They grip the cave roof with their toe claws and wrap their wings around themselves like blankets. When their food supply is scarce, some bats survive by hibernating. Their body temperatures plunge and their heartbeats slow down to eight pulses per minute. Bats can burn as much as 80 percent of their body fat during hibernation. So don't disturb a hibernating bat; just the act of waking up can cause the bat to burn a few weeks' supply of energy— enough to prevent it from surviving the winter.

Activity

FAT INSULATES Fat and fur are a mammal's key to surviving the cold winter. Whether or not a mammal hibernates, it's still important to maintain a constant body temperature. Try this. Take two glasses of warm water and wrap one with a towel. Secure the towel with a rubber band and place both glasses in the refrigerator for an hour. Check the temperature of the water. Dip your fingers into each glass. Which is warmer? Why?

Mammal or Not?

The late afternoon sun is hot, and the heat shimmers up from the African desert sands, making the huge termite mounds seem to jiggle and sway. Night is beginning to fall, bringing a hint of coolness. Nocturnal animals begin to stir. Inside the mound, the termite queen is busy laying eggs while the worker insects bustle around her bringing food, caring for the eggs, or making the nest strong and safe.

Nearby, you stop. There is something moving underground. Using your sensitive audio equipment, you scan the sand. Your equipment picks up a series of digging sounds as well as clicks, squeaks, and high-pitched grunts.

Quickly, you dig down deep into the sand, and you are rewarded. An odd-looking, pink, soft, wrinkly animal with a few prickly hairs writhes and waves its four legs in the air. Its skin is so loose that the animal can twist around inside it. Sharp claws almost cut you. This creature is strong! And it has sharp-looking mouth parts, too.

You release it, and it digs into the sand. Slowly, you uncover the intricate burrow. Tunnels are filled with these creatures that seem to move easily both forward and backward.

One of the animals is larger than the rest. It is a female, and she is giving birth. Tiny, pink creatures wriggle free of her as you watch, then make their way to her nipples to nurse. The others take care of the babies, bring the mother food, and dig.

Examining a couple of these creatures, you discover they have low body temperatures. Their temperatures exactly match the temperature of the burrow.

After you've finished scribbling your notes, you replace the sand and head back to camp, eager to figure out exactly what kind of animal you have found.

Animals can be classified, or organized into different species. Each kind of animal group has certain characteristics, but sometimes the lines blur. Your mystery animal shares qualities of many animals. Based on your observations and the information in the clue envelope, determine what kind of animal you've discovered.

Clues

INSECTS

- Some species live in complex social groups
- Sometimes have a queen that is the only female to produce young
- Some other members of the group are workers
- Exothermic—bodies are same temperature as surroundings
- No backbone
- Six legs
- Three body segments

MAMMALS

- Hair
- Endothermic—regulate body heat so their temperature generally stays the same no matter the environment
- Give birth to live young
- Feed milk to babies
- Backbone
- Four legs

Answer on page 32

No Offense, but You Really Smell

Human beings have five senses, and they work pretty well to help us explore the world around us. But those senses work even better in other mammals. Wild and domestic cats have better vision. Bats have better hearing. And when it comes to sniff power, nobody can beat a bloodhound. It's the winner by a lot more than a nose. It can sniff you out from the tiniest trace—a hair clip, a shoelace. Even when you can't smell yourself, a bloodhound can. In fact, to a bloodhound, you reek. And that's a good thing. Bloodhounds are used in rescue work all over the world. They've located countless missing children and adults, even when human searchers have given up. To loving friends and families, bloodhounds are true heroes.

But what makes their sense of smell so superior?

First, you have to understand that mammals smell with the use of their olfactory (ohl-FAC-tory) cells. These cells are located in the nose, making up tissue called the olfactory membrane. A bloodhound's snout is much bigger than the average person's nose. Its olfactory membrane, covering 150 square centimeters, is 50 times bigger than ours. Compared to a bloodhound, we can hardly smell anything at all.

Bloodhounds don't forget a scent, either. You can walk into a kitchen and get a strong whiff of frying sausages, and a few minutes later you won't notice the odor anymore. Your nose gets used to the smell because of a powerful built-in odor block that humans have. Once we sense that something in our surroundings isn't a threat, we no longer notice it. But bloodhounds don't have this odor-blocking ability. For them, scents stay strong. On the trail, bloodhounds also keep their olfactory cells fresh by taking quick sniffs and then emptying their noses to give the olfactory cells a rest.

Another special feature bloodhounds have are their highly tuned receptor sites. These sites "lock on" to a certain scent, helping the hound identify it and stay with it. Bloodhounds happen to have lots of receptor sites that are specially tuned to human scents.

So what does a bloodhound smell, anyway, when he's hot on your trail? Well, your cells. They come off you in tiny pieces of skin and fall to the ground. "Invisible dandruff" is the way these bits are described by Hilda Onderdonk, who, with her husband, David, owns two bloodhounds and regularly helps in rescue work. "If there's any breeze, it'll get blown away. But sooner or later it gets caught in the grass or the bushes. This is a scent pattern, the way it falls, and a bloodhound trails that scent."

Believe it or not, you shed 50 million cells a day, along with plenty of sweat. Skin and sweat don't have much of a smell, but the bacteria on them do. They give you your own scent, which is as distinctive as a fingerprint. Even identical twins don't have the same scent.

To prove this, David Onderdonk did an experiment with a pair of identical twin girls. These two looked so much alike that, as babies, they had to go back to the hospital several times so their names could be checked against their footprint records. Their own parents finally insisted that one girl wear her hair short and the other long, just so they could be told apart.

The two girls walked across a golf course that had been used by golf players all day. The long-haired twin went to the left and hid. Mr. Onderdonk gave one of the bloodhounds her nightshirt to smell. Instantly, the dog dashed across the golf course, following the girl's trail perfectly. He found her without missing a beat.

Some scientists say that all that loose skin on a bloodhound's neck helps it follow a scent. As the dog puts its nose to the ground, the skin falls forward. This creates a cupping effect (see picture, above) that traps the smell for the dog and makes it even stronger. With all these special features, bloodhounds can follow a scent all the way to the end of the trail.

Activity

TAKE A SENSE TEST Try this classroom test to see if you can improve your mammalian senses. Put a blindfold on and then listen to sounds around you. Do you hear things you hadn't heard when you could see? Now have someone else give you an unidentified piece of fruit to eat while still blindfolded, but also while holding your nose. Does the fruit taste different when you can't see or smell it? Write down your observations from these experiments in your journal.

SAVING
THE FLORIDA PANTHER

The Florida panther is in trouble. This majestic cat, the largest of its kind in the eastern United States, is on the brink of disappearing forever. Like hundreds of other mammals around the world, the Florida panther is an endangered species. As of this writing, there are fewer than 60 of these animals left.

An animal may become endangered for a number of reasons. New human development and construction have drastically reduced the panther's habitat of forest and swamp. As its habitat shrinks, the panther has been forced to go into other areas to find food. Sometimes panthers try to cross highways and are killed by speeding cars and trucks. Others have been shot by hunters and farmers who mistakenly see them as a threat to humans. Pollution in the air and water has poisoned some panthers and made others ill; it has also damaged their immune systems and made them more susceptible to disease.

What is the state of Florida doing to try to save the panther? In 1995, the state Fish and Wildlife Service (FWS) released eight Texas cougars into the panther's habitat. The cougar is one of the panther's closest relatives, and experts hoped that the female cougars would breed with the male panthers and produce healthy young.

This kind of interbreeding has been going on among big cats and many other animals for a long, long time. Interbreeding expands the genetic pool and increases the chances that the offspring will be healthy and strong.

In 1996, three panther kittens were born. As other healthy kittens are born each year, the Florida panther's story looks more and more like it will have a happy ending. But for many other endangered mammals, the outcome is not so certain.

The Florida Panther at a Glance

DESCRIPTION: Member of cougar family; rust to gray coat, with white on chest, muzzle, and underbelly.

HABITAT: Upper dry lands and wetlands such as swamps and marshes.

DIET: Deer, wild hogs, small alligators, raccoons, and rodents.

SOCIAL BEHAVIOR: Females care for young; males live alone; most active at dusk and dawn when hunting.

OUTSTANDING TRAITS: Can reach 35 mph (56 kmh) for short spurts; sharp senses of smell and vision; famous for panther scream.

LIFE SPAN: 12–15 years in the wild.

Other Ways Florida Is Trying to Save the Panther

CAPTIVE BREEDING Ten panther kittens were removed from the wild in 1991 and 1992. In captivity, the kittens can be protected and cared for and, eventually, returned to the wild. Not entirely successful, this program has been recently put on hold.

RADIO TRACKING Most of the panthers were briefly captured and equipped with radio collars that give off electronic signals. These collars allow humans to track the panthers' movements. The information they receive about the panthers' behavior and lifestyle can be invaluable in trying to save them.

PARTNERSHIPS WITH PRIVATE LANDOWNERS While some panthers live on public lands, such as Everglades National Park, others range over private lands that are quickly being developed. The state has offered money and other economic incentives to private landowners to keep their land in a natural state so it can remain a habitat for the panther and other wild animals.

Call of the Wild

A growing number of people are enjoying jobs that involve wildlife. In the U.S., most of these people work at the 500 government wildlife refuges, which allow animals to roam freely in areas specifically maintained for their needs. Many new careers center on coping with the effects on wildlife of pollution and deforestation.

Want to work outside? Consider work as an outdoor recreation planner. They coordinate the use of refuge land and waters, in addition to planning nature walks and visitor education programs.

Love law? A wildlife conservation officer enforces laws regarding hunting, trapping, and fishing. The conservation officer patrols a district in search of law breakers and assists in the prosecution of criminal charges against violators.

A growing field of concern is extinction. Biologists with the U.S. Fish and Wildlife Service help create recovery plans for the more than 700 plant and animal species in danger of dying out.

MAMMAL

Bizarre and Beautiful Noses

Star-nosed mole—This nearly blind mammal uses its nose to find food. ·····························>

Elephant seal—The male elephant seal can inflate his nose to twice its size to frighten away enemies and catch the eye of a female.

Elephant—It's a nose, it's a hand, and it's an arm! This versatile organ helps an elephant eat, drink, communicate, and smell.

THE TOOTH OF THE MATTER

Walrus—Males use their tusks as weapons to battle each other for females. Tusks also are used by hunters to hoist walruses out of the icy waters onto the ice.

Narwhal—The narwhal's teeth have adapted to become a long, swordlike horn.

EARS TO YOU

Elephant—The biggest of the big, these jumbo flaps keep the elephant cool. They're good for communicating, too. Flapping ears mean "Go away!"

Bat—Bats use sonar, or high-pitched sounds, to find insects and make their way around in the dark. They send out high-pitched tones that bounce off objects and echo back. Bats' ears pick up the returning sounds.

Hare—Big ears keep this desert mammal cool by allowing heat to dissipate.

Big Eaters

- An adult giant anteater can consume 30,000 termites in a day.
- An average bat can devour 4,000 flying insects in a night.
- The common mole eats nearly its own weight in insects and worms every day.
- An elephant eats up to 50 tons (45 m. tons) of its grassy environment each year.
- A platypus can eat 1,400 earthworms, 50 freshwater crayfish, and 40 tadpoles in one night.

mania

A **principal** walked into a classroom and saw a **chimpanzee** sitting at a desk writing. "Why, that's **extraordinary!**" exclaimed the principal.

"Oh, I don't know," said the teacher. "You should see how atrocious his **spelling** is!"

The Truth About Mammals

- Many species of bats are vegetarians—or fruitarians. The bulk of the others eat insects. There are, however, a couple of species that feed on animals. The tiny vampire bat of Latin America makes a small incision just above the hoof on a cow's leg and then laps up the blood with its tongue, like a cat drinking milk. It rarely attacks humans.

- Pigs like to wallow in mud because it cools them off and protects them from the sun. A pig's skin is very sensitive and can sunburn easily.

- Outdoor laborers in India protect themselves from tiger attacks by wearing masks on the backs of their heads. Tigers attack only from behind and will not attack a man that is "facing" them!

ED: What's worse than a GIRAFFE with a sore throat?

FRED: AN ELEPHANT with a runny nose.

MISNAMED MAMMALS

- The koala is not a bear but a marsupial.
- The spiny anteater is not an anteater, although it does eat ants.
- The sea cow is not a cow.
- The maned wolf is actually a fox.
- The flying fox is actually a bat.
- The killer whale and the pilot whale are both dolphins.

Q: What is a monkey's favorite month?
A: Ape-ril.

UNUSUAL NAMES FOR MAMMAL GROUPS

A CLOWDER OF CATS
A SKULK OF FOXES
A TROOP OF KANGAROOS
A PRIDE OF LIONS
A KINE OF COWS

A PACE OF DONKEYS
A SLEUTH OF BEARS
A POD OF SEALS
A CARAVAN OF CAMELS
AN AMBUSH OF TIGERS

Final Project:
The Last Living Mammal

You've now read all about mammals and how far they've come, how they've adapted, and their amazing diversity. It's time to ask, "What would the world be like without them?"

Assume that there occurs a sudden major catastrophe. Pick one from the list at right or make up your own. Assume that whichever one you pick will result in the total destruction of all mammals except one species. Your job is to tell which species has survived. Is it the biggest, strongest, smallest, or most intelligent? Just what critter will be the last mammal on Earth? Perhaps it's the one most like other classes of animals, such as insects, reptiles, and fish. Maybe it's an animal we now consider a pest. Or, maybe a marine mammal. What will these animals encounter in this post-apocalyptic world? What will be the effect of their offspring on the food chain? What habitats and ecosystems will they find? What adaptations might they undergo?

Write your findings in a special edition of a newspaper that will be published in a small colony on Mars where humans have taken refuge. Your headline should be "The Last Living Mammal," and your article should explain what led up to the extinction of the rest of the mammals on Earth—and what is predicted to happen next.

▶ The polar ice caps melt, flooding Earth's surface.

▶ An asteroid strikes Earth. Depending on its location—land, ocean, or one of the poles—the results would vary.

▶ A volcanic eruption blocks out the sun.

▶ Disease wipes out plant life.

▶ Famine or disease wipes out all orders of mammals but one, which is resistant.

ANSWERS

Solve-It-Yourself Mystery, page 24: The animal is a mammal—technically, at least. It is an actual animal called the naked mole rat, and it lives underground in African deserts. Naked mole rats have hair, four legs, and give birth to live young. Sounds like a mammal? Right. But they live like insects. There is a queen, and she is the only female that mates, reproduces, and nurses the babies with milk. A small group of breeding males mate with her. The other animals are workers, like worker termites or worker bees. Each has its own role to play in the colony; some tend to the babies, some dig the burrow, and others find food.

Mammals are endothermic, or warm-blooded. But naked mole rats are exothermic. Their body temperatures are determined greatly by the environment. Insects are exothermic, too. So how did scientists decide to classify the naked mole rat as a mammal? Two words: hair and milk. Only mammals have hair, and only mammals nurse their babies with milk.